School Buses

by Dee Ready

Content Consultant:
Karen E. Finkel, Executive Director
National School Transportation Association

Bridgestone Books

an imprint of Capstone Press

Bridgestone Books are published by Capstone Press
818 North Willow Street, Mankato, Minnesota 56001
http://www.capstone-press.com

Library of Congress Cataloging-in-Publication Data
Ready, Dee.
    School buses/by Dee Ready.
    p. cm.
    Includes bibliographical references and index.
    Summary: Describes a school bus and its different parts, including the lights, stop arm,
back door, and mirrors.
    ISBN 1-56065-612-3
    1. School buses--Juvenile literature. [1. School buses.] I. Title.
TL232.R37   1998
629.222'33--dc21

                                        97-12197
                                          CIP
                                           AC

Photo credits
Michelle Coughlan, 16
Betty Crowell, 4
FPG/Jeffrey Sylvester, 20
International Stock/Scott Barrow, 6
Unicorn Stock, 12; Karen Holsinger Mullen, 8, 10, 18; Martha McBride, 14;
    Dennis Mac Donald, cover

Table of Contents

School Buses

School buses carry children to school.
They bring children home from school.
Sometimes school buses take children
on field trips. A field trip is a visit to
see things and learn.

Mirrors

Mirrors are fixed onto a school bus. The mirrors help the driver see around the school bus. They help the driver see children and other cars. Mirrors help make the bus safe.

Yellow Lights

School buses have flashing yellow lights on the outside. Flashing means the lights turn on and off very fast. Two yellow lights are on the front of the bus. Two yellow lights are on the back. These lights tell other drivers that the bus is stopping.

Red Lights

School buses also have flashing red lights on the outside. Two red lights are on the front of the bus. Two red lights are on the back. These lights tell drivers to stop and wait. The lights flash until the bus starts moving again.

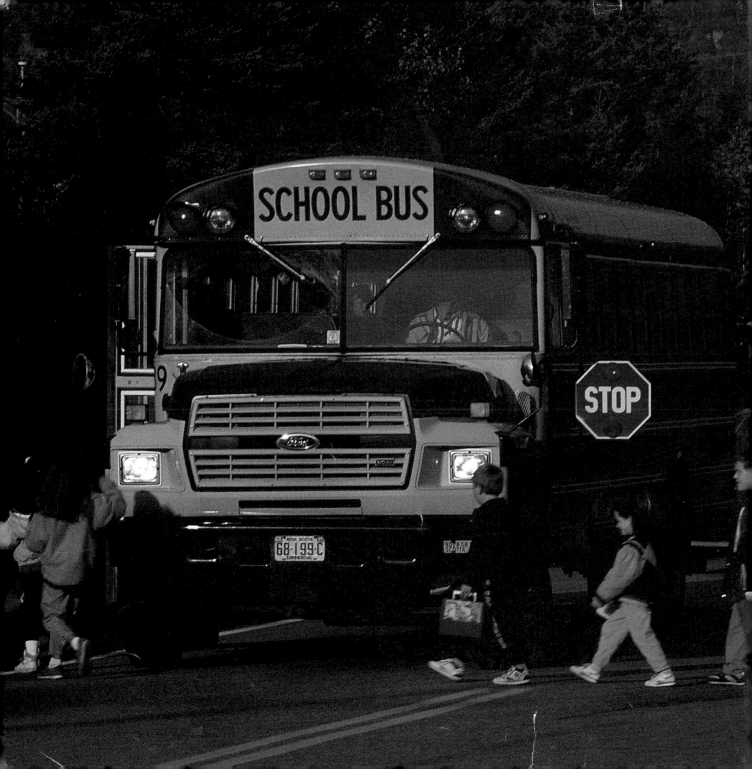

Stop Sign

Every school bus has a stop sign. The stop sign is on the side of the bus. The sign sticks out when the bus door is open. It folds against the bus when the door is closed.

Front Door

Children use the front door to enter the bus. They use the front door to leave the bus. The bus driver opens the door. This makes the stop sign come out. Then cars stop. This way children can enter or leave the bus safely.

Seats

School buses have two rows of seats. An aisle runs between the seats. An aisle is a walkway between seats. Some school buses have as many as 22 seats. A school bus can hold many children.

Windows

School buses have many windows. Each
seat is next to a window. Sometimes the
top part of the window can be opened.
The windows are small to help keep
children safe. Children should keep
their heads and arms inside the bus.

SCHOOL BUS

EMERGENCY DOOR

P

FLORIDA
COUNTY 92479

230

ward 230

Back Door

Most school buses have back doors. The back door is used in an emergency. An emergency is a sudden danger. It could be a fire or a crash. The back door makes it easier to get off the bus.

Hands On: Be Safe on the Bus

There are rules for riding school buses.
Following the rules will make your bus ride
a safe one.

- Be on time for your bus.
- Stand back from the road.
- Make sure the bus has stopped before you move.
- Look for cars.
- Always cross in front of the bus. Wait for the driver to tell you when to cross.
- Never crawl under a school bus.
- Stay in your seat.
- Always follow the driver's orders.
- Do not play with the back door. It is only for an emergency.

Words to Know

aisle (EYE-uhl)—the walkway between seats

emergency (i-MUR-juhn-see)—a sudden danger like a fire or crash

field trip (FEELD TRIP)—a visit to see things and learn

flashing (FLASH-ing)—turning on and off very fast

Read More

Chlad, Dorothy. *Riding on a Bus*. Chicago: Children's Press, 1985.

Crews, Donald. *School Bus*. New York: Greenwillow Books, 1984.

Nichols, Paul. *Big Paul's School Bus*. Englewood Cliffs, N.J.: Prentice-Hall, 1981.

Ready, Dee. *School Bus Drivers*. Mankato, Minn.: Bridgestone Books, 1998.

Internet Sites

Safety Bear's School Bus Safety
http://www.dps.state.ak.us/AST/safety/scholbus.htm
School Bus Safety and School Transportation
http://www.stnonline.com

Index